Redrawing the Order: China's Pursuit of Superpower Status and Its Impact on International Norms

Ann Chen & Grey Wang

ISBN: 9798388690012

Dedicated to all those who seek to understand the complex and ever-evolving role of China in the global order. May this book inspire informed and thoughtful discourse on the opportunities and challenges presented by China's pursuit of superpower status, and encourage greater cooperation and collaboration among nations to build a more just, peaceful, and sustainable world.

CONTENTS

ACKNOWLEDGMENTS

I would like to express my sincere gratitude to everyone who has contributed to the making of this book. First and foremost, I would like to thank my family for their unwavering love and support throughout the process. Additionally, I would like to thank the countless experts and scholars whose insights and research have informed this book. Their tireless efforts and contributions to the field of China studies are truly remarkable, and have greatly inspired me in my own research and writing.

1 INTRODUCTION: CHINA'S RISE AND GLOBAL IMPLICATIONS

In recent decades, China's rise has been one of the most significant geopolitical and economic developments in the world. With a population of over 1.4 billion people and a rapidly growing economy, China is on track to become a superpower and play a dominant role in shaping the global order. China's rise has brought about significant changes in the world, and its impact is likely to continue to be felt for decades to come.

This chapter aims to provide an overview of China's rise and its global implications. It will begin by examining the factors that have contributed to China's rise and the challenges it has faced along the way. It will then analyze the various ways in which China's rise is impacting the world, including geopolitics, the global economy, global security, and cultural norms.

Factors Contributing to China's Rise
China's rise has been fueled by several factors. One of the most significant has been its economic growth. Since China began implementing economic reforms in the late 1970s, its economy has grown at an unprecedented rate, with an average annual growth rate of over 9 percent. This rapid growth has led to an increase in China's global economic power, making it the world's second-largest economy after

the United States.

Another factor contributing to China's rise has been its growing military power. China has been investing heavily in its military in recent years, and it has become increasingly assertive in its territorial claims in the South China Sea and other regions. China's military expansion has raised concerns among its neighbors and other countries in the region.

China's rise has also been supported by its large population and human resources. With a population of over 1.4 billion people, China has a vast pool of human resources that it can draw upon for economic and military development. Additionally, China has a highly educated population, with a large number of scientists, engineers, and other skilled professionals.

Challenges to China's Rise

Despite its impressive rise, China faces several challenges that could impact its ability to become a superpower. One of the most significant challenges is its aging population. China's one-child policy, which was in place for several decades, has resulted in an aging population that could have significant economic and social implications. Additionally, China faces environmental challenges, including pollution and climate change, that could impact its economic growth and social stability.

Another challenge to China's rise is its relationship with other countries, particularly the United States. The U.S. and China have been engaged in a strategic competition, with each country seeking to exert its influence in the world. This competition has led to increased tensions and the potential for conflict between the two countries.

Global Implications of China's Rise

China's rise is having significant global implications across several domains, including geopolitics, the global economy, global security, and cultural norms.

Geopolitics

China's rise is shifting the balance of power in the world, challenging the dominant position of the United States. China's growing economic and military power has allowed it to expand its influence in Asia and beyond, and it has become more assertive in its territorial claims in the South China Sea. China's rise has also led to the development of new alliances and partnerships, as countries seek to align themselves with China or the United States.

The Global Economy

China's rise is also having a significant impact on the global economy. China is now the world's largest trading nation and a major player in international finance. Its growing economic power has led to the development of new global economic institutions, such as the Asian Infrastructure Investment Bank and the New Development Bank. China's economic policies, including its Belt and Road Initiative, are reshaping global trade patterns and investment flows.

Global Security

China's military expansion is raising concerns about global security, particularly in the Asia-Pacific region. China's growing military power and territorial ambitions have led to tensions with its neighbors, including Japan, South Korea, and Taiwan. China's territorial claims in the South China Sea have also raised concerns among other countries in the region, as well as the United States, which has been conducting freedom of navigation operations in the area. China's growing military power has also led to the development of new military technologies, including hypersonic missiles and advanced cyber capabilities. This has raised concerns among other countries about the potential for a new arms race and increased instability in the world.

Cultural Norms

China's rise is also having an impact on global cultural norms. China's soft power, including its rich history, cultural traditions, and economic success, is increasingly being felt around the world. Chinese films, music, and fashion are gaining popularity, and Chinese companies are becoming major players in global markets.

However, China's rise has also raised concerns about its influence on global values and norms, particularly with regard to human rights and democracy. China's one-party system and restrictions on freedom of expression have been criticized by human rights advocates and some countries, and its growing influence in international institutions has raised questions about the future of global governance.

China's rise is reshaping the global order and has significant implications for the world. While China's economic and military power is growing, it also faces several challenges, including an aging population and environmental issues. The competition between China and the United States is also a significant factor shaping the global landscape. As China continues to pursue superpower status, it will be essential for the world to navigate the challenges and opportunities that arise from this process. This book will examine the various ways in which China's rise is impacting the world and explore potential strategies for managing this change in a way that promotes cooperation and stability.

3 CHINA'S BELT AND ROAD INITIATIVE: IMPLICATIONS FOR GLOBAL INFRASTRUCTURE

The Belt and Road Initiative (BRI), launched by Chinese President Xi Jinping in 2013, is an ambitious plan to connect Asia, Europe, and Africa through a network of roads, railways, ports, and other infrastructure projects. The initiative aims to promote economic development, regional integration, and cultural exchange among the participating countries. As China's most significant foreign policy and economic strategy in recent years, the BRI has far-reaching implications for global infrastructure development and international norms.

The BRI is divided into two main components: the Silk Road Economic Belt, which connects China to Europe through Central Asia, and the 21st Century Maritime Silk Road, which links China to Southeast Asia, South Asia, the Middle East, and Africa through a series of ports and maritime routes. These two components encompass over 60 countries, accounting for about 65% of the world's population and 30% of global GDP. The initiative has been met with both enthusiasm and skepticism, as countries weigh the potential benefits and risks of participating in China's grand vision.

One of the most significant implications of the BRI is the massive investment in infrastructure projects across the participating countries. China has pledged to invest over $1 trillion in the initiative, with the Asian Infrastructure Investment Bank (AIIB) and the Silk Road Fund providing additional financial support. These investments have the potential to address the significant infrastructure gap in many developing countries, particularly in Asia and Africa, where the need for new roads, railways, ports, and energy facilities is immense. By providing much-needed financing and technical expertise, the BRI could help to spur economic growth and improve living standards in these regions.

However, the BRI also raises concerns about the potential for debt dependency and environmental degradation. Many of the participating countries are already heavily indebted, and the influx of Chinese loans could exacerbate their debt burdens. Critics argue that China's lending practices lack transparency and often come with strings attached, such as the requirement to use Chinese contractors and labor. This has led to accusations of "debt-trap diplomacy," whereby China uses its financial leverage to gain political influence and control over strategic assets, such as ports and natural resources.

Moreover, the environmental impact of the BRI's infrastructure projects is a significant concern. Many of the community to engage with China and ensure that its economic policies are transparent, sustainable, and in line with international norms and standards.

5 CHINA'S MILITARY EXPANSION: IMPLICATIONS FOR GLOBAL SECURITY

China's military expansion and modernization efforts have been a source of concern for many countries around the world, particularly the United States and its allies in the Asia-Pacific region. As China continues to grow in economic and political power, it is also seeking to enhance its military capabilities to protect its interests and project power beyond its borders. This chapter will explore China's military expansion and its implications for global security. One of the key drivers of China's military expansion is its territorial disputes in the East and South China Seas. China claims sovereignty over the majority of the South China Sea, including islands and reefs that are also claimed by several other countries, such as Vietnam, the Philippines, and Malaysia. In the East China Sea, China and Japan have conflicting claims over the Senkaku/Diaoyu Islands. These disputes have led to increased tensions and occasional clashes between Chinese and other countries' naval and air forces.

To assert its claims and protect its interests in these disputed areas, China has been building up its military capabilities, particularly its naval and air forces. China has invested heavily in the development of new naval vessels, including aircraft carriers, destroyers, and submarines, and has been expanding its naval presence in the South China Sea and beyond. China has also been developing advanced weapons systems, such as anti-ship missiles and stealth aircraft, which could potentially threaten the US military and its allies in the region.

China's military expansion has also been driven by its desire to play a more prominent role in global affairs. As China's economic and political influence has grown, it has sought to increase its military capabilities to match its status as a major world power. China has been increasing its military spending and modernizing its armed forces to develop a more capable and sophisticated military. For example, China has been investing in advanced technologies such as artificial intelligence, space-based capabilities, and cyber warfare.

The growth of China's military capabilities has led to concerns among many countries, particularly the United States and its allies in the region. The US has been strengthening its military presence in the Asia-Pacific region, including through the deployment of new weapons systems such as the Terminal High Altitude Area Defense (THAAD) missile defense system in South Korea. The US has also been increasing its military cooperation with other countries in the region, such as Japan, South Korea, and Australia, to counter China's growing military capabilities.

China's military expansion also has implications for global security, particularly in the context of nuclear weapons. China is one of the five recognized nuclear-weapon states under the Nuclear Non-Proliferation Treaty (NPT), and it is believed to have the world's second-largest nuclear arsenal after the US. China's nuclear weapons capabilities have been growing, and it has been developing new nuclear weapons systems, including hypersonic missiles and submarine-launched ballistic missiles. The growth of China's nuclear capabilities could potentially destabilize the global strategic balance, particularly if it leads to an arms race with the US and other countries.

Moreover, China's military expansion and modernization efforts raise concerns about its strategic intentions. Some analysts argue that China's growing military capabilities are part of a broader effort to challenge US dominance in the Asia-Pacific region and establish China as the preeminent power in the region. Others suggest that China's military expansion is driven by a desire to protect its economic and strategic interests and ensure its national security.

China's military expansion and modernization efforts have significant implications for global security. The growth of China's military capabilities, particularly in the context of its territorial disputes and its desire to play a more prominent role in global affairs, has raised concerns among many countries, particularly the US and its allies in the

Asia-Pacific region. The development of advanced weapons systems, including nuclear weapons, also has the potential to destabilize the global strategic balance.

Another aspect of China's military expansion that has raised concerns is its increasing assertiveness in territorial disputes. China has been involved in territorial disputes with several neighboring countries, including Japan, Vietnam, the Philippines, and India, over the sovereignty of islands and maritime boundaries in the East and South China Seas. China has pursued an aggressive strategy to assert its claims, including the construction of artificial islands, the deployment of military assets, and the establishment of air defense identification zones. This assertiveness has led to heightened tensions and increased the risk of military conflict in the region. The United States, which has treaty obligations to defend Japan and the Philippines, has responded by increasing its military presence and engagement in the region, including freedom of navigation operations in the disputed waters. The potential for a military clash between the United States and China in the region is a significant concern, given the potential for escalation and the destabilizing impact it could have on the global economy and security.

China's military expansion also has significant implications for global arms control and non-proliferation efforts. China is rapidly modernizing its nuclear and conventional military capabilities, including the development of new technologies such as hypersonic missiles and anti-satellite weapons. China's nuclear arsenal is estimated to consist of about 350 warheads, a fraction of the United States and Russia's arsenals but still a significant number.

China's military modernization, particularly in the nuclear realm, has raised concerns about the potential for a new arms race and the destabilizing impact it could have on global security. China's increasing military capabilities could also prompt other countries, particularly in the region, to pursue their own military buildup or seek closer ties with the United States, leading to a further escalation of tensions and the potential for conflict.

China's military expansion has significant implications for global security and the balance of power in the international system. China's pursuit of superpower status and its growing military capabilities are reshaping the dynamics of the Asia-Pacific region and challenging the United States' traditional role as the dominant power. The potential for conflict and destabilization is high, particularly in the context of ongoing territorial disputes and geopolitical rivalries. As China continues to expand its military capabilities and assert its influence, it will be essential for the international community to engage with China to manage tensions and promote stability in the region and beyond.

6 THE UNITED STATES-CHINA STRATEGIC COMPETITION AND ITS IMPACT ON THE GLOBAL ORDER

In recent years, the strategic competition between the United States and China has become one of the most consequential issues for the global community. The two countries are the largest economies in the world and have vastly different political systems, ideologies, and approaches to governance. The competition between these two global powers has significant implications for the global order, as well as for individual countries and regions around the world.

The roots of the US-China strategic competition can be traced back to the early 2000s when China began to rapidly emerge as a global economic power. While the United States has been the dominant global superpower since the end of World War II, China's rapid rise has challenged the existing power structure. This competition has intensified in recent years, as both countries have engaged in a tit-for-tat trade war and strategic rivalry in areas such as technology, military, and influence in the Asia-Pacific region.

One of the key areas where the US-China competition is playing out is in the economic realm. The two countries have the largest and second-largest economies in the world, respectively. The US has traditionally been the dominant economic power, but China's rise has disrupted this status quo. The US has accused China of engaging in unfair trade practices, intellectual property theft, and currency manipulation. These accusations have led to the imposition of tariffs and other trade barriers, which have had a significant impact on the global economy.

The US-China strategic competition is also playing out in the military realm. The two countries have vastly different military capabilities, with the US having the largest and most technologically advanced military in the world, while China has been rapidly modernizing and expanding its military capabilities. The two countries have engaged in a strategic rivalry in areas such as the South China Sea, Taiwan, and North Korea. The US has accused China of engaging in aggressive behavior and violating international norms, while China has accused the US of interfering in its internal affairs and engaging in provocative military maneuvers.

Another area where the US-China strategic competition is having a significant impact is in the technological realm. Both countries are leading players in the development and deployment of new technologies such as artificial intelligence, 5G, and quantum computing. The US has accused China of engaging in intellectual property theft and forced technology transfer, while China has accused

7 THE QUAD ALLIANCE AND ITS SIGNIFICANCE FOR THE ASIA-PACIFIC REGION

The Quad Alliance is a group consisting of four nations: the United States, Japan, India, and Australia. It was formed in 2007 as a response to the growing concerns about China's rising influence in the Asia-Pacific region. The Quad is viewed as a strategic partnership and aims to promote a free and open Indo-Pacific region, maintain a rules-based international order, and enhance economic and security cooperation.

The Quad's significance lies in its ability to counter China's growing influence in the Asia-Pacific region. China has been rapidly expanding its economic and military presence in the region, which has raised concerns among other nations. The Quad aims to provide a balance of power in the region and prevent any one country from dominating it. One of the most significant impacts of the Quad is its ability to enhance economic cooperation among its member nations. The Quad has identified several areas of economic cooperation, including infrastructure development, digital connectivity, and supply chain resilience. These efforts could help create new opportunities for businesses and entrepreneurs, while also promoting economic growth and development in the region.

The Quad is also significant in terms of its military capabilities. The alliance is working to enhance military cooperation, including joint military exercises and sharing of intelligence. This is an important step in building a more cohesive defense strategy in the region, and could help prevent conflict or aggression from other nations.
The Quad's focus on maintaining a rules-based international order is another key aspect of its significance. China has been criticized for its actions in the South China Sea, including building artificial islands and claiming territorial rights over the area. The Quad aims to promote a peaceful resolution to these conflicts, while also upholding the principles of international law and freedom of navigation.

Another important impact of the Quad is its potential to promote democratic values in the region. All four member nations are democratic countries, and the Quad aims to promote the principles of democracy, human rights, and the rule of law. This could help counter China's authoritarian approach and promote a more open and free society in the Asia-Pacific region.

The Quad's significance can be seen in its ability to promote regional stability and security. The alliance aims to enhance maritime security and prevent illegal activities, such as piracy and smuggling. This could help create a more stable and secure environment for all nations in the foreign language, both within China and abroad. By promoting Chinese language and culture, China aims to increase its global influence and to establish itself as a leading cultural and economic power.

China has also been investing in the media and entertainment industries as a means to promote its soft power. Chinese films, music, and television shows are increasingly popular not only within China but also in other parts of the world. China has been investing in the production of high-quality media content that showcases Chinese culture and values, in order to influence global cultural norms and promote a positive image of China. In addition to promoting its own culture, China has been engaging in cultural diplomacy, through which it seeks to build relationships with other countries through cultural exchanges and collaborations. China has been sponsoring cultural events, such as the Confucius Institute and the Belt and Road Initiative, as a means to promote Chinese culture and to establish cultural ties with other countries. These efforts have been aimed at promoting understanding and mutual respect between China and other countries, and at projecting China as a responsible and reliable global partner.

China's soft power efforts have had a significant impact on global cultural norms. China's rising influence in the world has led to increased interest in Chinese culture and language, and Chinese cultural exports have become increasingly popular in many parts of the world. This has had a significant impact on global cultural norms, as China's cultural values and traditions have become more widely known and accepted.

At the same time, China's soft power efforts have faced criticism and skepticism from some quarters. Some critics have argued that China's promotion of its own culture is aimed at promoting Chinese influence and dominance, rather than at promoting global cultural exchange and understanding. Others have raised concerns about China's use of cultural diplomacy as a means to influence political and economic outcomes in other countries.

China's soft power strategies have had a significant impact on global cultural norms in recent years. China's promotion of its own culture, language, and media content has increased global interest in Chinese culture and has helped to shape global perceptions of China's rise. However, China's soft power efforts have also faced criticism and skepticism from some quarters, and there are concerns about the use of cultural diplomacy as a means to influence political and economic outcomes. Overall, China's soft power strategies will continue to be an important factor in shaping global perceptions of China's rise and its impact on international norms.

9 THE CHALLENGE OF HUMAN RIGHTS IN CHINA'S RISE TO SUPERPOWER STATUS

The rise of China to superpower status is one of the most significant geopolitical events of the 21st century. While China's economic and military might is well-documented, its human rights record has been a constant source of international concern. The challenge of human rights in China's rise to superpower status raises important questions about the compatibility of authoritarianism and democracy, and the role of human rights in global governance.

China's human rights record has been a subject of international criticism for decades. China has been accused of a range of human rights abuses, including censorship, suppression of free speech, religious persecution, forced labor, and repression of ethnic minorities. While China has made some progress in addressing some of these issues, many argue that the situation has only worsened in recent years. The Chinese government's response to the COVID-19 pandemic, including its initial cover-up of the outbreak and suppression of dissenting voices, has been a particularly notable example of China's human rights abuses.

The challenge of human rights in China's rise to superpower status raises important questions about the compatibility of authoritarianism and democracy. China's rise has been accompanied by an increase in authoritarianism, with the government tightening its grip on power and cracking down on dissent. At the same time, the rise of China has coincided with a decline in the influence of liberal democracies, raising concerns about the future of democratic governance. The question of whether authoritarianism or democracy is better equipped to address the challenges of the 21st century is one of the most important debates of our time.

The challenge of human rights in China's rise to superpower status also raises important questions about the role of human rights in global governance. As China becomes more influential on the global stage, there is a risk that it will use its power to promote its own values and interests at the expense of human rights. This is particularly concerning given China's poor human rights record. The international community must find ways to balance China's growing influence with the need to uphold human rights and democratic values.

In recent years, there have been some signs of progress in addressing the challenge of human rights in China's rise to superpower status. The international community has taken steps to hold China accountable for its human rights abuses, including sanctions and other forms of pressure. The United States, in particular, has taken a more assertive stance towards China's human rights record under the Biden administration. At the same time, there have been efforts to engage with China on human rights issues, with some arguing that dialogue and engagement are more effective than sanctions.

Ultimately, the challenge of human rights in China's rise to superpower status is one of the most complex and pressing issues of our time. As China becomes more influential on the global stage, it is imperative that the international community finds ways to hold China accountable for its human rights abuses while also engaging with it on issues of mutual concern. The role of human rights in global governance must be reaffirmed and strengthened, and democratic values must be upheld as essential to the future of the global order.

10 THE ROLE OF TECHNOLOGY IN CHINA'S RISE AND ITS IMPLICATIONS FOR THE GLOBAL ORDER

The rise of China as a global power has been accompanied by a rapid expansion of its technology sector. Over the past two decades, China has emerged as a leading player in the fields of telecommunications, artificial intelligence, and quantum computing, among others. The country's rapid technological advancement has implications not only for China's domestic economy but also for the global order. In this chapter, we will examine the role of technology in China's rise to superpower status and the implications of this trend for the global economy and international relations.

One of the key drivers of China's technological advancement has been the government's focus on innovation and investment in research and development. In recent years, China has increased its spending on R&D, surpassing the United States in overall spending. This investment has allowed China to develop new technologies and products, particularly in areas such as 5G wireless technology and quantum computing.

China's technological advancements have allowed the country to emerge as a global leader in several key sectors. For example, Chinese technology companies such as

Huawei and ZTE have become major players in the global telecommunications industry. Huawei, in particular, has been at the forefront of the development of 5G wireless technology, which is expected to revolutionize the way people connect and communicate in the coming years. China's increasing technological prowess has also raised concerns among other countries, particularly the United States. In recent years, the US government has taken steps to limit Chinese access to sensitive technologies, citing national security concerns. The US has also accused China of engaging in intellectual property theft and other unfair trade practices, which has led to an ongoing trade dispute between the two countries.

The rise of China's technology sector also has implications for the global economy. Chinese technology companies are increasingly competing with established firms in the United States and other developed countries. This competition has led to concerns about job losses and economic displacement in these countries. At the same time, the growth of China's technology sector has also created new opportunities for collaboration and partnership between Chinese and international firms.

China's growing role in the global technology sector has also raised concerns about the country's influence over the development of international technology standards. As Chinese firms become more influential in global markets, they may seek to shape the rules and standards governing these markets in their favor. This could lead to tension between China and other countries, particularly the United States and other Western nations.

Overall, the role of technology in China's rise to superpower status is complex and multifaceted. On the one hand, China's technological advancements have allowed the country to become a leading player in several key sectors and have driven economic growth and innovation. On the other hand, China's growing influence in the global technology sector has raised concerns about national security and economic competition, as well as the potential for China to shape international norms and standards in its favor. The implications of this trend for the global order are likely to be far-reaching and will require careful consideration by policymakers and scholars in the years to come.

11 CHINA'S ENVIRONMENTAL FOOTPRINT AND ITS IMPLICATIONS FOR GLOBAL SUSTAINABILITY

China's rapid economic growth over the past few decades has had a significant impact on the environment, both within the country and globally. With the world's largest population and the second-largest economy, China's environmental footprint is substantial, and its actions have significant implications for global sustainability. This chapter will explore China's environmental footprint, the actions the country has taken to address environmental issues, and the potential implications of China's environmental policies for global sustainability.

China's environmental footprint is significant and multifaceted, covering issues such as air and water pollution, waste management, and climate change. Rapid industrialization and urbanization have led to high levels of air pollution in many cities, particularly in the north, where coal is the primary energy source. Water pollution is also a major concern, with many rivers and lakes contaminated by industrial waste and agricultural runoff. In addition, China's massive waste generation, particularly in its cities, has strained the country's waste management infrastructure.

Recognizing the severity of these environmental issues, China has taken significant steps in recent years to address them. In 2013, the government announced a "war on pollution," pledging to tackle air and water pollution through a range of policy measures, including closing polluting factories and reducing coal consumption. China has also invested heavily in renewable energy, becoming the world's largest investor in renewable energy sources such as solar and wind power. Additionally, China has implemented a series of policies to encourage sustainable practices, such as the establishment of an emissions trading system and the promotion of eco-cities and green buildings.

The impact of China's environmental policies on global sustainability is complex and multifaceted. On the one hand, China's commitment to renewable energy and sustainable development is a positive step towards reducing global greenhouse gas emissions and mitigating the impacts of climate change. By investing in renewable energy and promoting sustainable practices, China is helping to drive down the cost of renewable energy technologies, making them more accessible to other countries. In addition, China's investments in green technologies are creating new industries and jobs, which could help drive economic growth and development.

However, China's environmental policies also have some negative implications for global sustainability. For example,

China's heavy reliance on coal has resulted in high levels of carbon emissions, which contribute to global climate change. While China is investing heavily in renewable energy, it is still the world's largest consumer of coal, and the shift away from coal is likely to take time. Additionally, some of China's policies to promote sustainability, such as the establishment of eco-cities, have been criticized for being more about image than substance, with some projects failing to meet sustainability targets.

Furthermore, China's role in global resource consumption also has significant implications for global sustainability. As the world's largest consumer of raw materials, China's demand for resources such as timber, metals, and minerals has contributed to deforestation, habitat loss, and other environmental problems in other parts of the world. Additionally, China's investments in infrastructure and development in other countries, particularly in Africa, have led to concerns about environmental degradation and unsustainable practices.

China's environmental footprint is significant and has implications for global sustainability. While China has taken steps to address environmental issues, there is still a long way to go. The impact of China's environmental policies on global sustainability is complex and multifaceted, with both positive and negative implications. It is important for China to continue to invest in sustainable practices and to work collaboratively with other countries to address global environmental challenges.

12 THE FUTURE OF THE WORLD TRADE ORGANIZATION IN LIGHT OF CHINA'S RISE

The World Trade Organization (WTO) was established in 1995 to promote free trade and resolve trade disputes among member countries. It operates on the principles of non-discrimination, transparency, predictability, and the promotion of fair competition. With China's rise as a global economic powerhouse, the WTO is facing new challenges that will require innovative solutions to ensure its continued relevance and effectiveness.

China's accession to the WTO in 2001 marked a turning point in the global economy. Its entry into the world's largest trading bloc provided an unprecedented opportunity for China to access new markets, while also exposing the country to the norms and rules of the international trading system. Over the past two decades, China has become the world's largest exporter and second-largest importer, with its economic growth fueled by global trade. However, China's rapid rise has also challenged the existing rules and norms of the WTO.

One of the main challenges to the WTO is China's approach to industrial policy. China's state-led economic model, which includes massive government subsidies, has enabled Chinese companies to dominate key industries such as steel, aluminum, and solar panels. This approach has been criticized by other countries, who argue that it distorts competition and violates WTO rules. The United States has been particularly critical of China's industrial policies and has imposed tariffs on Chinese goods in response.

Another challenge to the WTO is China's role in the digital economy. China is home to some of the world's largest technology companies, such as Alibaba and Tencent, and has rapidly developed its own digital ecosystem. However, China's digital policies have raised concerns among other countries, who argue that China's restrictions on foreign technology companies and data localization requirements violate WTO rules. The United States has also accused China of stealing intellectual property and engaging in cyber espionage.

In addition to these challenges, China's Belt and Road Initiative (BRI) has raised questions about the WTO's ability to regulate global trade. The BRI is a massive infrastructure project that aims to connect China with Europe, Asia, and Africa through a network of railways, highways, ports, and pipelines. However, the BRI has been criticized for its lack of transparency, environmental concerns, and potential debt traps for developing countries. Critics argue that the BRI is part of China's broader strategy to reshape the global economic and political order.

To address these challenges, the WTO will need to adapt to the changing global economic landscape. One option is to negotiate new rules that take into account China's unique economic model and digital policies. For example, the WTO could establish new rules on state-led industrial policies, or create a new set of rules for digital trade. Another option is to reform the WTO's dispute settlement system, which has been hampered by a lack of resources and political will. The WTO could also work with other international organizations, such as the International Monetary Fund and the World Bank, to address issues related to the BRI.

China's rise as a global economic powerhouse has presented new challenges to the WTO. China's approach to industrial policy, digital policies, and the BRI have raised questions about the effectiveness of the existing rules and norms of the WTO. To remain relevant and effective, the WTO will need to adapt to these new challenges by negotiating new rules, reforming its dispute settlement system, and working with other international organizations to address global trade issues.

13 CHINA'S DIPLOMATIC STRATEGY AND ITS IMPLICATIONS FOR INTERNATIONAL RELATIONS

China's rise to superpower status has been accompanied by a transformation of its diplomatic strategy. As it expands its influence and assertiveness on the global stage, China's diplomatic approach has shifted from a low-key and defensive posture to a more proactive and assertive one. This chapter examines China's diplomatic strategy and its implications for international relations.

China's diplomatic strategy is multifaceted, with various components such as economic diplomacy, soft power diplomacy, and military diplomacy. One of the most prominent aspects of China's diplomatic strategy is its Belt and Road Initiative (BRI), which seeks to build infrastructure and deepen economic ties across Asia, Europe, Africa, and beyond. By financing and building roads, railways, ports, and other infrastructure projects, China aims to strengthen its economic ties with other countries and increase its geopolitical influence.

Another aspect of China's diplomatic strategy is its use of soft power to win over foreign public opinion and influence international discourse. China has invested heavily in cultural and educational exchanges, and it promotes Chinese culture and language through Confucius

Institutes and other initiatives. It has also sought to portray itself as a champion of global governance and a responsible stakeholder in the international system.

At the same time, China's diplomatic strategy has become more assertive and confrontational in recent years. This is particularly evident in its approach to territorial disputes in the South China Sea and the East China Sea. China has aggressively asserted its territorial claims, constructing military bases on artificial islands and engaging in naval standoffs with its neighbors. China has also sought to leverage its economic power to pressure other countries into complying with its demands, as seen in its recent economic coercion against Australia and other countries.

China's diplomatic strategy has significant implications for international relations. Its BRI projects have raised concerns about debt sustainability, environmental impact, and the potential for China to use its economic leverage to extract political concessions. Its assertive behavior in territorial disputes has raised concerns about potential military conflict and instability in the region. Its use of economic coercion has raised concerns about the potential for other countries to become more dependent on China and more vulnerable to its pressure.

China's diplomatic strategy has also led to increasing tensions with other major powers, particularly the United

States. As China seeks to challenge American dominance in the global order, the two countries have engaged in a series of economic and geopolitical competitions, ranging from trade tensions to military posturing in the South China Sea. The future trajectory of China's diplomatic strategy will have significant implications for the future of international relations and the global order.

China's pursuit of superpower status has been accompanied by a transformation of its diplomatic strategy. While it has sought to use economic and soft power diplomacy to build influence and win over foreign public opinion, it has also become more assertive and confrontational in its approach to territorial disputes and economic coercion. China's diplomatic strategy has significant implications for international relations, including potential conflict and instability, concerns about debt sustainability and environmental impact, and the future trajectory of the global order.

14 CHINA'S INFLUENCE IN AFRICA AND ITS IMPLICATIONS FOR GLOBAL DEVELOPMENT

China's growing influence in Africa has been a significant area of study and concern for many analysts in recent years. China has become one of the biggest investors and trading partners with African countries, and this has raised questions about the implications of this relationship for global development. This chapter will explore China's growing influence in Africa, the motivations behind China's engagement in Africa, and the implications of China's growing influence in Africa for global development.

China's Engagement in Africa

China's engagement with Africa has increased significantly in recent years. According to the China Africa Research Initiative (CARI), a research project at the Johns Hopkins School of Advanced International Studies, China's trade with Africa has increased from $10 billion in 2000 to $190 billion in 2017. China has also become a significant investor in African countries. From 2005 to 2018, China's total foreign direct investment (FDI) in Africa was over $100 billion.

One of the key features of China's engagement with Africa is the Belt and Road Initiative (BRI), which aims to connect China to Europe, Asia, and Africa through a series of infrastructure projects. The BRI has been a significant source of funding for African countries, with China investing in several infrastructure projects in Africa, including railways, ports, and airports. This has allowed African countries to improve their infrastructure and boost economic growth.

Motivations Behind China's Engagement in Africa
China's engagement with Africa is driven by a range of economic, political, and strategic interests. China views Africa as an important source of natural resources, particularly oil and minerals, which are critical for China's economic development. Africa is also a growing market for Chinese products and services, providing opportunities for Chinese companies to expand their operations and increase their profits.

China's engagement in Africa is also motivated by political and strategic interests. China has been working to increase its global influence and challenge the dominance of the United States. Africa is seen as an important region for China to increase its global influence, particularly given Africa's growing importance in the global economy.
Implications of China's Influence in Africa for Global Development
China's growing influence in Africa has significant implications for global development. On the one hand, China's engagement with Africa has provided much-needed investment and infrastructure for African countries, which

has helped to boost economic growth and development. This has been particularly important for African countries that have struggled to attract investment from other countries.

However, there are also concerns about the implications of China's growing influence in Africa. Some analysts have raised concerns about the impact of Chinese investment on African countries' debt levels, as many African countries have borrowed heavily from China to finance infrastructure projects. There are also concerns about the impact of Chinese investment on local industries and employment, as Chinese companies often bring in their own workers and equipment.

China's engagement with Africa has also raised questions about the role of China in the global economy and its impact on global development. Some analysts have raised concerns about China's use of its economic power to advance its political interests, which could undermine global development efforts. There are also concerns about the impact of China's engagement in Africa on global governance, as China's growing influence in Africa could challenge the dominance of Western countries in global governance institutions.

China's growing influence in Africa has significant implications for global development. While China's engagement with Africa has provided much-needed investment and infrastructure for African countries, there are also concerns about the impact of Chinese investment on African countries' debt levels and local industries. China's engagement with Africa has also raised questions about the role of China in the global economy and its impact on global governance.

15 THE TAIWAN STRAIT AND ITS IMPACT ON CHINA'S REGIONAL INFLUENCE

The Taiwan Strait is a narrow body of water separating Taiwan and China, and it has long been a contentious issue in East Asia. The People's Republic of China (PRC) claims Taiwan as a province of China and seeks eventual reunification with the island, while Taiwan sees itself as an independent, sovereign state. The dispute over Taiwan has implications not only for cross-strait relations but also for the wider region, particularly as China continues to rise as a superpower.

One of the primary reasons for China's insistence on reunification with Taiwan is its desire to maintain its territorial integrity and national sovereignty. The Communist Party of China (CPC) views Taiwan as a renegade province that must be brought back under Chinese control, and it has repeatedly stated that any attempt at formal independence by Taiwan would be met with force. This stance has led to tensions between China and the United States, which has a long-standing commitment to Taiwan's defense and has sold weapons to the island to help it deter a potential Chinese invasion.

The Taiwan Strait issue has also had implications for China's regional influence. As China's economy has grown and its military capabilities have expanded, some analysts have suggested that China's ultimate goal is to become the dominant power in East Asia, pushing the United States out of the region and establishing a Sino-centric order. The Taiwan Strait is seen as a key test of China's ability to project power in the region and to challenge American dominance.

The Taiwan issue has also been used by China to build ties with other countries in the region. China has sought to isolate Taiwan diplomatically, pressuring countries to sever diplomatic relations with Taiwan and instead recognize the PRC as the sole representative of China. This strategy has been largely successful, with most countries in the region now recognizing the PRC rather than Taiwan. In addition, China has used economic ties to build influence in the region, offering trade and investment deals to countries that are willing to distance themselves from Taiwan.

Despite these efforts, the Taiwan issue remains a significant challenge for China's regional influence. The United States remains committed to Taiwan's defense, and Taiwan has developed a formidable military, including advanced missile systems that could threaten China's coastline. In addition, Taiwan has developed a vibrant democracy and a strong civil society, which have won it significant international support. China's aggressive stance toward Taiwan has also raised concerns among its neighbors, many of whom fear that China's assertiveness could lead to conflict in the region.

16 CHINA'S DISINFORMATION AND CYBERSECURITY STRATEGIES AND THEIR IMPLICATIONS FOR THE GLOBAL ORDER

China's use of disinformation and cybersecurity strategies has become a growing concern for the global order. The Chinese government has been accused of using disinformation campaigns to influence public opinion, manipulate international media, and even interfere in other countries' elections. Additionally, China's growing capabilities in cybersecurity have raised concerns about its potential use for espionage, theft of intellectual property, and sabotage of critical infrastructure.

One of China's most notable disinformation campaigns was its attempt to downplay the severity of the COVID-19 outbreak in Wuhan, which was first reported in late 2019. The Chinese government initially censored news about the outbreak and downplayed its significance, which allowed the virus to spread quickly and ultimately become a global pandemic. Additionally, Chinese state media outlets spread disinformation about the virus, including conspiracy theories that it was created in a US military lab. This disinformation campaign allowed China to deflect blame for its mishandling of the outbreak and shift the narrative away from its own responsibility.

China's cybersecurity capabilities have also raised concerns among the international community. The Chinese government has been accused of using cyber espionage to steal intellectual property and trade secrets from foreign companies. Additionally, China has been accused of using cyberattacks to disrupt critical infrastructure, such as power grids and transportation systems. The potential consequences of such attacks could be devastating, causing widespread disruptions to daily life and potentially endangering lives.

The Chinese government has also been working to increase its control over the internet within its borders. The Great Firewall of China, a censorship system that blocks access to certain foreign websites and social media platforms, is one example of this effort. The government has also implemented laws that require tech companies operating within China to store user data within the country and provide backdoor access to authorities. These measures have raised concerns about the government's ability to monitor and control online activity within China, as well as its potential to extend this control beyond its borders.

The implications of China's disinformation and cybersecurity strategies are significant for the global order. China's efforts to shape public opinion, interfere in elections, and influence the media threaten the integrity of democratic institutions and the free flow of information.

Its cybersecurity capabilities raise concerns about the potential for espionage, theft, and sabotage on a global scale. Additionally, China's control over the internet within its borders and its potential to extend that control beyond its borders could limit free expression and have a chilling effect on political dissent.

In response to China's actions, many countries have been taking steps to improve their own cybersecurity capabilities and increase their resilience to disinformation campaigns. Additionally, international organizations such as NATO and the EU have been working to develop strategies for countering disinformation and improving cybersecurity. The United States, in particular, has been working to increase international cooperation on cybersecurity issues and has been pressuring China to improve its behavior in this area.

Overall, China's use of disinformation and cybersecurity strategies is a major challenge for the global order. As China continues to rise in power and influence, it will be important for the international community to work together to address these issues and prevent them from undermining the stability and security of the global order.

17 THE ROLE OF INTERNATIONAL LAW IN CHINA'S RISE TO SUPERPOWER STATUS

China's rise to superpower status has been accompanied by a growing interest in international law. As China has become more active on the global stage, it has increasingly turned to international law to advance its interests and shape the rules of the international system. This chapter explores the role of international law in China's rise to superpower status, examining how China has used international law to achieve its goals, as well as the challenges and opportunities that China's engagement with international law presents for the international community.

China's approach to international law is shaped by its historical experience and its self-perception as a great power. China has a long history of engaging with international law, dating back to the late Qing dynasty when China began to participate in the international legal system. However, China's experience with international law has not always been positive. In the 19th and early 20th centuries, China was forced to sign a series of unequal treaties that ceded significant amounts of territory and sovereignty to foreign powers. This experience has left a lasting legacy on China's approach to international law, with China often viewing the international legal system with suspicion and mistrust.

Despite this historical legacy, China has become an increasingly active participant in the international legal system in recent decades. China has acceded to numerous international treaties and agreements and has played an active role in international organizations such as the United Nations and the World Trade Organization. China has also sought to use international law to advance its interests, particularly in areas such as maritime disputes in the South China Sea and the Belt and Road Initiative.

China's use of international law has been characterized by a mix of cooperation and confrontation. On the one hand, China has sought to work within the existing legal framework to advance its interests. For example, China has pursued a strategy of legalizing its territorial claims in the South China Sea through the use of international law, particularly the United Nations Convention on the Law of the Sea (UNCLOS). China has also been an active participant in the World Trade Organization, using the organization to advance its economic interests and promote its vision of economic globalization.

On the other hand, China has also been willing to challenge existing international norms and rules when they conflict with its interests. China's approach to the South China Sea disputes is a case in point. China has rejected the jurisdiction of international tribunals in the South China Sea and has sought to advance its territorial claims through a combination of military assertiveness and diplomatic pressure. Similarly, China has been criticized for its human rights record and its treatment of ethnic and religious minorities, with some arguing that China's actions violate international human rights norms and standards.

China's engagement with international law presents both challenges and opportunities for the international community. On the one hand, China's increasing participation in the international legal system has the potential to strengthen the system and promote the rule of law globally. China's active engagement with the World Trade Organization, for example, has helped to promote economic liberalization and global trade. Similarly, China's participation in the United Nations has helped to promote global cooperation on issues such as climate change and peacekeeping.

On the other hand, China's use of international law to advance its interests has also raised concerns among some in the international community. Critics argue that China's approach to international law is driven by a desire to assert its power and influence, rather than a commitment to the rule of law. Others argue that China's actions in areas such as the South China Sea and human rights are undermining the credibility of the international legal system and eroding global norms and standards.

China's engagement with international law is a complex and multifaceted phenomenon that reflects both China's growing power and influence on the global stage and its historical legacy and self-perception as a great power.

18 THE CHALLENGE OF MANAGING CHINA'S RISE FOR INTERNATIONAL COOPERATION

As China continues its rapid economic and military rise, it poses a significant challenge to the international community in terms of managing its ascendancy in a way that preserves global stability and promotes cooperation. China's growing power and assertiveness have caused concerns among other nations, particularly the United States, about its intentions and potential threat to the existing international order. This chapter will examine the challenges of managing China's rise and the prospects for international cooperation in the face of this growing power.

One of the biggest challenges in managing China's rise is the lack of consensus among other nations about how to engage with it. Some countries view China as a strategic partner and are willing to engage in trade and investment to benefit from its economic growth. Others see China as a threat and seek to contain its influence, particularly in Asia. The United States, in particular, has taken a more confrontational approach, seeing China as a strategic competitor and seeking to limit its influence through various means, including trade tariffs, military alliances, and diplomatic pressure.

The challenge of managing China's rise is exacerbated by the lack of transparency in China's political system, particularly its military and security apparatus. China's Communist Party exercises tight control over the media and the internet, limiting access to information about its decision-making processes and internal workings. This lack of transparency creates uncertainty about China's intentions and actions, which can lead to mistrust and suspicion among other nations.

Another challenge is the divergence of values and norms between China and other countries, particularly those in the West. China's authoritarian political system and state-led economic model are at odds with the liberal democratic values that are prevalent in much of the world. This divergence creates challenges in areas such as human rights, intellectual property protection, and trade practices, which can lead to tensions and disputes between China and other nations.

The challenge of managing China's rise is also evident in the realm of cybersecurity. China has been accused of engaging in state-sponsored hacking and cyber espionage, which has led to concerns about the security of critical infrastructure and sensitive data. In addition, China's adoption of restrictive internet policies, such as the Great Firewall, has raised concerns about internet freedom and censorship.

Despite these challenges, there are opportunities for international cooperation in managing China's rise. One area of potential cooperation is in addressing global challenges such as climate change, terrorism, and pandemic diseases. China has the potential to play a significant role in these areas, and cooperation with other nations could help to build trust and promote stability.

Another area of potential cooperation is in economic integration. China's Belt and Road Initiative, which seeks to expand trade and investment along ancient trade routes, has the potential to create economic opportunities for many countries. However, concerns about debt sustainability and potential political influence have led some countries to view the initiative with skepticism. Greater transparency and consultation with other nations could help to address these concerns and promote greater cooperation.

Managing China's rise is a significant challenge for the international community. The lack of consensus about how to engage with China, the lack of transparency in its political system, the divergence of values and norms, and cybersecurity concerns are all factors that contribute to this challenge. However, there are also opportunities for cooperation in addressing global challenges and promoting economic integration. It will require careful navigation of these challenges and a willingness to engage in dialogue and cooperation to ensure that China's rise is managed in a way that promotes stability and benefits the global community.

19 CHINA'S RISE AND ITS IMPACT ON EMERGING MARKETS AND DEVELOPING COUNTRIES

China's rise to superpower status has had significant implications for the world, particularly for emerging markets and developing countries. China's massive economic growth over the past few decades has created a new world order in which China has emerged as a key player. This chapter will explore the impact of China's rise on emerging markets and developing countries, and the challenges and opportunities that this presents.

One of the most significant impacts of China's rise on emerging markets and developing countries has been its effect on trade. China is now the world's largest trading nation and has become a key trading partner for many countries in Asia, Africa, and Latin America. This has led to increased trade and investment flows between China and these regions, and has helped to drive economic growth in many emerging markets and developing countries.

However, China's rise has also had some negative impacts on these countries. Chinese exports have flooded many markets, leading to concerns about the impact on local industries and jobs. China's dominance in certain sectors has also made it difficult for other countries to compete, particularly in industries such as steel, textiles, and electronics.

China's rise has also had significant geopolitical implications for emerging markets and developing countries. China's growing influence in these regions has led to concerns about the impact on democracy, human rights, and the rule of law. Some countries have been wary of China's motives and have sought to balance their relationships with other powers such as the United States and Europe.

China's Belt and Road Initiative (BRI) is another important aspect of its rise and has had significant implications for emerging markets and developing countries. The BRI is a massive infrastructure development project that aims to connect China with Europe, Asia, and Africa through a network of roads, railways, and ports. While the BRI has the potential to bring significant economic benefits to many countries, it has also been criticized for being a debt trap and for promoting China's geopolitical interests.

China's rise has also had implications for the global governance system. As China has become more influential, it has sought to have a greater say in international organizations and to shape the rules and norms of the global system. This has led to tensions with other major powers such as the United States and Europe, who are concerned about China's increasing influence.

Finally, China's rise has also created opportunities for emerging markets and developing countries. China has become a major source of development finance, and its investments in infrastructure projects have helped to address the massive infrastructure deficit in many countries. China has also been a key partner in efforts to combat climate change, and its investment in renewable energy has helped to drive down the cost of renewable technologies and make them more accessible to developing countries.

China's rise to superpower status has had significant implications for emerging markets and developing countries. While it has created new opportunities, it has also created new challenges, particularly in terms of trade, geopolitics, and global governance. As China continues to rise, it will be important for the international community to work together to ensure that the benefits of China's rise are shared fairly and that the challenges are addressed in a way that promotes sustainable and inclusive development for all.

20 CONCLUSION: THE FUTURE OF THE GLOBAL ORDER IN LIGHT OF CHINA'S PURSUIT OF SUPERPOWER STATUS

China's pursuit of superpower status and its impact on international norms has had a significant impact on the global order. The rise of China as a global power has fundamentally changed the balance of power in the world, challenging the dominance of the United States and other Western powers.

China's approach to international relations has been marked by a focus on economic growth and expansion, which has led to an increase in its influence in developing countries and emerging markets around the world. However, this approach has also brought with it a number of challenges, particularly in the areas of human rights, democracy, and international law.

In order to manage China's rise to superpower status, the international community will need to engage with China in a constructive and productive manner. This will require a willingness to engage with China on a range of issues, from economic and trade policies to human rights and democracy. It will also require a willingness to work with China on issues of global concern, such as climate change and nuclear proliferation.

At the same time, the international community must be prepared to hold China accountable for its actions, particularly when it comes to human rights violations and aggressive territorial claims. The United States and other Western powers have an important role to play in this regard, but they must be willing to engage with China in a constructive and productive manner, rather than resorting to confrontational tactics that could lead to conflict.

Ultimately, the future of the global order will depend on the ability of the international community to navigate the complex and evolving relationship between China and the rest of the world. It will require a willingness to engage with China in a way that is both respectful and assertive, and that seeks to promote the common interests of all nations. If the international community can rise to this challenge, it is possible that the rise of China could lead to a more stable and prosperous global order.

ABOUT THE AUTHOR

Ann Chen and Grey Wang are promising young scholars with a keen interest in international relations and China studies. They are both undergraduate students majoring in Political Science and have demonstrated a passion for understanding the complexities of China's rise as a global superpower.

Despite their young age, Ann and Grey have already made significant contributions to the field of international relations. They have conducted extensive research on China's Belt and Road Initiative, and have presented their findings at a number of academic conferences and symposia.

Ann and Grey's work has been recognized for its insight and rigor, and has earned them accolades from their peers and professors. They are both committed to pursuing graduate studies and careers in academia, with the goal of advancing our understanding of the world and promoting greater global cooperation.

Printed in Great Britain
by Amazon